WHAT'S IT LIKE TO BE A..?

CHOREOGRAPHER

Elizabeth Dowen   Lisa Thompson

First published in the UK 2010 by
A & C Black Publishing Ltd
36 Soho Square
London
W1D 3QY
www.acblack.com

Copyright © 2009 Blake Publishing
Published 2009 by Blake Education Pty Ltd, Australia

ISBN: 978-1-4081-2875-6

Written by Lisa Thompson and Elizabeth Dowen
Publisher: Katy Pike
Editor: Eve Tonelli
Cover Design: Terry Woodley
Designer: Matt Lin and Clifford Hayes
Printed and bound in China by Leo Paper Products.

Cover image © Shutterstock/AYAKOVLEVdotCOM

All inside images © Shutterstock except p15 (b)-Rick Rycroft, AP,
p16 (m)–Clemens Bilan, AFP, p16 (b)–AP, p17 (t)–Paul Kolnik, AFP, p17
(m)–Steven Caras, AP, p17 (bl, br)–Tracey Nearmy, AAP image, p23
(b)–AFP, p31 (t)–The Benesh Institute, Royal Academy of Dance, London

With grateful thanks to Mr Ashley Killar, Director of the Ecole Ballet and
Dance Theatre, Sydney.

This book is produced using paper made from wood grown in managed,
sustainable forests. It is natural, renewable and recyclable. The logging and
manufacturing processes conform to the environmental regulations of the
country of origin.

All the Internet addresses given in this book were correct at the time of
going to press. The author and publishers regret any inconvenience caused
if addresses have changed or sites have ceased to exist, but can accept no
responsibility for any such changes.

Contents

TIME TO MOVE!

R RISE DANCE STUDIO

I love being first here, before the day begins.

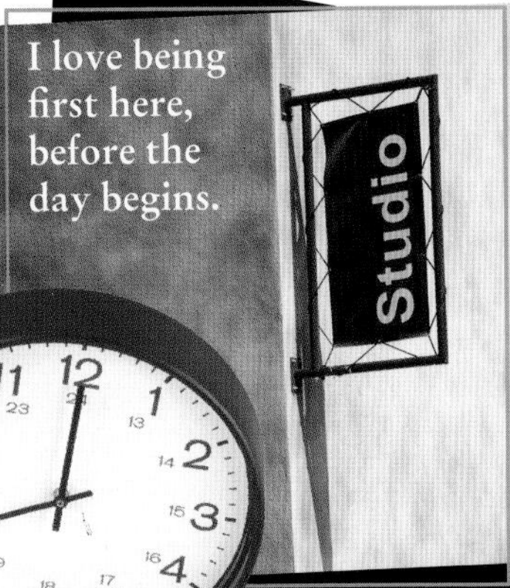

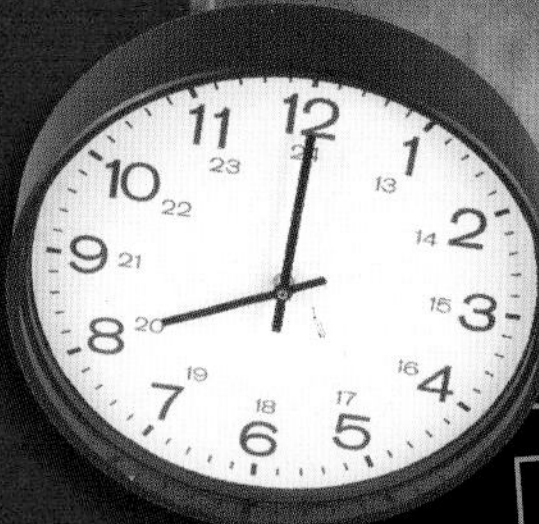

It is 8 am when I arrive at my dance studio. I don't have classes to teach until after lunch, so I have been using my mornings to choreograph three dances for the upcoming annual Festival of the Sea, which my dance group, Rise, is participating in.

For the dances, I commissioned music from three very different, young, local musicians to reflect 'a day in the life of a beach'. I have been playing the pieces over and over since I received them two weeks ago. I have worked out nearly all the dance phrases and sequences. I play the music again as I stretch and prepare to dance.

my chosen musicians

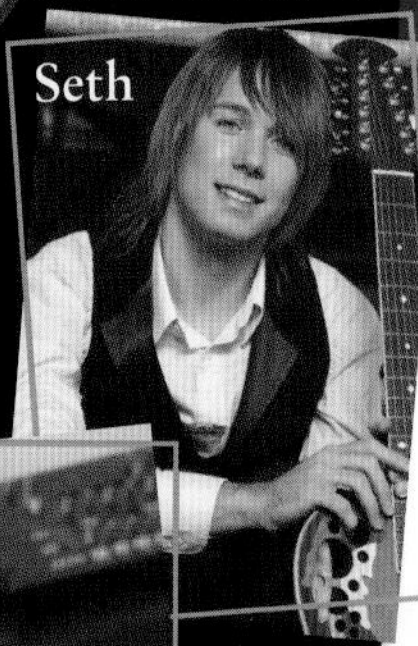

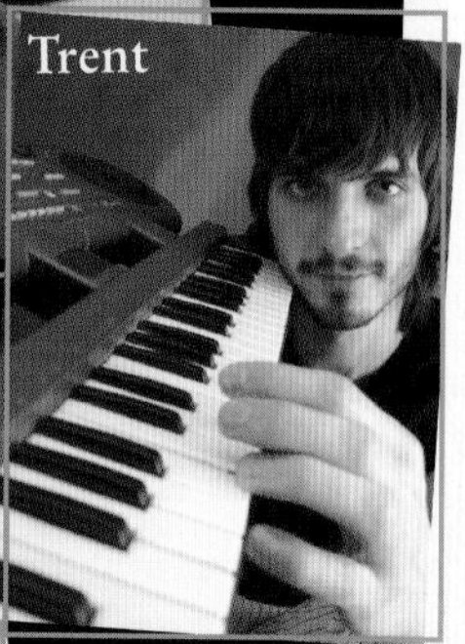

Seth

Monique

Trent

Warming up is essential for dancing.

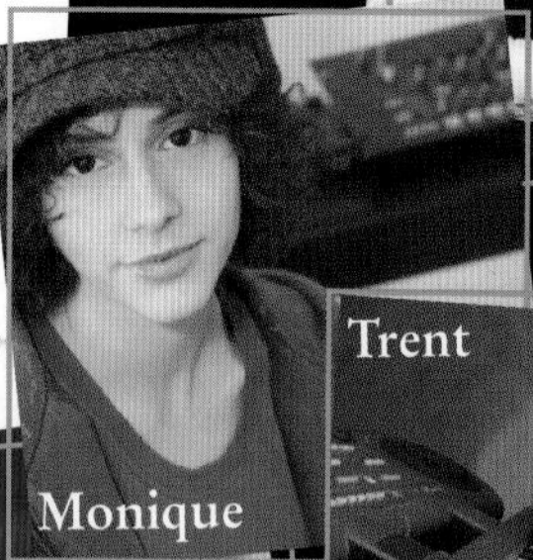

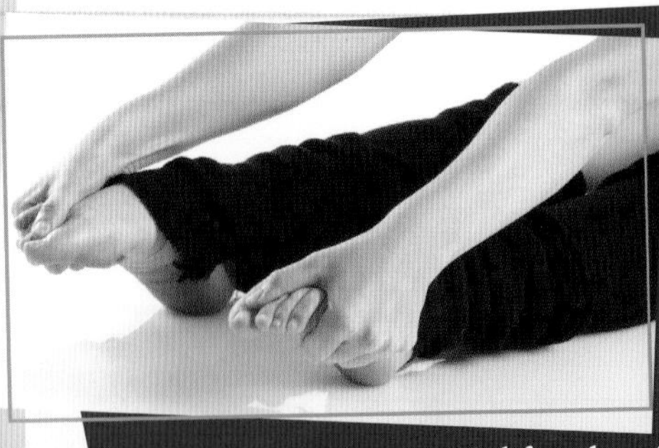

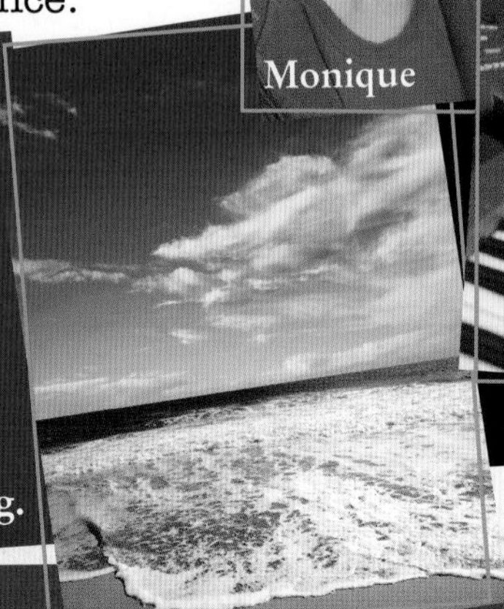

I begin to dance to the music, trying out the steps and movements I have imagined. Some of them work – and some don't. I continue to dance all morning, improvising, taking notes, listening and letting my body move and create. I jump, step, repeat movements, and slowly the dances come together.

I'm trying to picture the dance in my mind.

Getting the beat right is so important.

I'm excited – the movements and the music are blending together better than I could have hoped. I can't wait to show my dancers the moves this afternoon so we can begin rehearsing.

How will it look with all my dancers together?

Improvise:
to compose, perform or deliver without previous preparation; to create on the spur of the moment.

Right, what's the show date again?

With the festival only six weeks away, there is so much to prepare behind the scenes too – staging, costumes, lighting and props. It's going to be a very busy time!

How I became a choreographer

Check out these young ballroom dancers!

I was just like these little girls.

a dance school show

I have always loved to dance and perform. When I was four years old, I started ballet and jazz lessons at a local dance school.

I always enjoyed performing at the end of year concerts. I was so excited at the thought of being on stage in front of my family and friends. I can still remember the thrill I got from showing them the dances I had learnt.

At high school, I carried on taking dance classes in the evenings and on weekends. I would make up dances with my friends for fun. That's when the choreographing bug bit me! I also kept performing at festivals and dance competitions.

Festivals were so much fun.

I liked the costumes too.

I went on to study dance and human movement at a performing arts college, and successfully auditioned for a small dance company called Wicked Moves when I graduated. It was a contemporary dance company that toured around the country.

I made some great friends at college and on tour.

After five years of touring, I formed my own contemporary dance school, and now I choreograph and teach. While I do miss the buzz of performing, I still spend most of my time dancing.

Being able to artistically realise a dance and see it performed is fantastic. Creating dances can be lots of work, but it is very rewarding and it's what I love to do. There really is nothing else like creating dance – for me it's the ultimate in creativity and freedom.

It is a dream come true to have my own studio.

Starting young

Most professional classical dancers have studied ballet from about the age of five. However, some modern dancers, particularly men, can begin training as late as 16–20 years old.

Being creative is the key.

What does a choreographer do?

Just as a writer tells a story or expresses an idea using words, a choreographer translates stories, ideas and moods into dance movements and sequences for dancers to perform.

Moves created here ...

... end up performed here.

Choreographers create dance routines for all kinds of performances – for stage, TV or film performances, music videos, fashion shows or corporate events. Choreographers also work as movement coaches for actors.

fashion shows

stage shows

Choreographers need excellent communication skills to explain their ideas. Dancers follow a choreographer's instructions, so they need to understand what the choreographer wants them to do.

Like me, very few people earn enough money from choreography alone. Most choreographers are also teachers, dancers or company artistic directors.

Teaching can be very rewarding.

SKILLS NEEDED TO BE A CHOREOGRAPHER

- a passion for dance
- excellent physical fitness
- strong spatial and body kinaesthetic awareness
- excellent leadership abilities
- a very quick 'eye' to analyse moves
- high level of focus
- excellent organisational skills
- ability to handle pressure
- determination to succeed

passion for dance

be fit

Tasks can involve:

- developing ideas and turning them into a finished performance
- choosing music
- planning movements to fit music
- auditioning and selecting dancers
- teaching and rehearsing dances
- meeting with producers, costume designers, musical and artistic directors
- recording the steps on paper or film.

DIDYOUKNOW?

A WORD ABOUT DANCE

The word *choreography* comes from the Greek words *choros*, meaning *dance*, and *graphia*, meaning to *write down*.

doing the hard work

Meetings are part of the job.

DANCE through the ages

Throughout history, people have expressed ideas, stories and emotions by moving their bodies.

There are dancers on this 5th century Greek vase.

This stone tablet shows a dancer from ancient Mexico.

Evidence of early dance, such as artefacts and cave paintings, shows that among ancient societies, dance was one of the first arts. It existed long before written language. Dance was mainly for ritual purposes, such as praying to the gods, celebrating events or victories, connecting spiritually with ancestors, and telling stories.

18th century Shaker believers dancing

Sioux Native Americans dancing in the 19th century

Xochipilli

ANCIENT DANCERS

In ancient Greek mythology, Terpsichore was the goddess of dancing.
The Hindu god Shiva takes the form of Nataraja (Lord of the Dance) and performs a dance of creation and destruction.
The Aztecs of Mexico had a god called Xochipilli who was a god of music, love, flowers and dance.

These dancing Muslims are called Whirling Dervishes.

10

As human communities became more complex, dancers became highly valued as performers. Those who created dances long ago used the same raw material that choreographers use today – the human body.

a Pacific Islander performing

modern dance

Over the centuries, dance has evolved into a broad range of different movements and styles all over the world. These styles are constantly changing as new dances are created.

EXAMPLES OF DANCE STYLES

Some of the main dance categories are:

- tap
- jazz
- ballet – e.g. classical or contemporary/modern
- ballroom – e.g. waltz, foxtrot
- Latin American – e.g. mambo, tango, samba
- street – e.g. hip hop, breakdancing
- swing – e.g. rock 'n' roll, jive
- folk dancing – e.g. maypole dancing, clogging.

DID YOU KNOW?

THAT'S A LOT OF SHOES

For some professional ballet dancers, pointe shoes only last a performance or two.

ballroom moves

breakdancing

dancing around a maypole

THE BODY AS AN }INSTRUMENT

A choreographer brings a dance to life through the bodies of their dancers. Many dances focus on a particular part of the body for expression.

HEAD

In many Indian and South-East Asian dances, the head is an important part of the dance. The head, eyes, eyebrows and mouth are all used to help tell the story of the dance.

The head and face are most important in Indian Kathakali dancing.

Asian fan dancing

ARMS

Most dances use the arms. Arm movements can be strong, graceful, percussive, vibrating or flowing.

ELBOWS

In many European folk dances, dancers place their hands on their hips so that their elbows point out to the sides. Couples may also link arms and spin each other around.

HANDS

Dancers from South-East Asian cultures spend countless hours learning the dozens of hand shapes and gestures of their dances. Movements vary from being slow and controlled to trembling and frenzied.

The hands say it all.

folk dancers in a spin

STOMACH
Skilful belly dancers can make their stomachs shake and ripple.

Ballerinas make the most of their legs.

LEGS
The legs give the body its movement. Often, it is what the legs do that defines the range of movement on stage.

KNEES
Many indigenous dances use the half–squat position to emphasise the angles of the knees and to create sharp, percussive movements.

This African dance involves the knees.

CHOREOGRAPH THIS!
Although used mainly for dance, choreography is also used in:
- gymnastics
- figure skating
- cheerleading
- marching bands
- synchronised swimming
- stage combat (fight choreography)
- and many other activities involving movement.

figure skating

FEET
Foot stomping and the way feet hit the ground are an expressive and defining part of dance – from the elegant glide of a ballet dancer, or the tap of a tap dancer, to the stamp of the flamenco.

tap-dancing feet

DIDYOUKNOW?

THE POWER OF DANCE

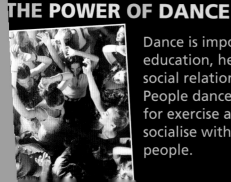

Dance is important in education, health and social relationships. People dance for fun, for exercise and to socialise with other people.

The World of dance

Almost every culture has a dance form of its own. Some date back thousands of years, while others have been created more recently to express new ideas. Energetic, soulful, political, educational or playful, all these dances bring people together.

Here are just a handful of the hundreds of dance styles from around the world.

rock 'n' roll

English Morris dancing

North America

Native American dances, e.g. Inuit drum dances (Canada)
foxtrot, jazz, rock 'n' roll, disco, hip hop (USA)
hula (Hawaii)

Caribbean

limbo (Trinidad)
mambo (Cuba)
salsa (Caribbean)

hip hop

Argentinean tango

South America

samba (Brazil)
morenada (Bolivia)
tango (Argentina and Uruguay)

spinning morenada

Europe

highland dancing (Scotland)
Morris dancing (England)
cancan (France)
flamenco, paso doble (Spain)
waltz (Austria)

polka (Czech Republic/
Slovakia/Central Europe)
ballet (Italy)
sirtaki/hora (Greece)
Chukchi traditional
dancing (Russia)

a Greek Hora performance

a Russian Chukchi dancer

Bollywood-style dancing in India

Asia

belly dancing (Middle East)
classical dances (India)
Bollywood style dancing (Mumbai,
India)
Nihon Buyo (Japan)
sword and dragon dances (China)

traditional Chinese
sword dancing

Africa

San/Bushmen trance-like dances (South
Africa)
soukous/African rumba (Congo)
Maasai 'Adumu' (jumping) dance (Kenya/
Tanzania)

Maasai
warriors'
jumping
dance

Australia

indigenous (Aboriginal)
Dreamtime dancing
Bush dancing

Aboriginal dancing

Maasai warriors' jumping dance

New Zealand

the Haka – an indigenous (Maori)
group dance

the Haka

FAMOUS
CHOREOGRAPHE[R]

MARTHA GRAHAM 1894–1991

Martha Graham was an American dancer who becar[me] of the most well-known choreographers of the 20th c[entury] and a pioneer of contemporary dance. She invented a[...] dance style which was raw and emotional, rather tha[n] the dreamlike, glamorous dancing that had gone befo[re]. Her technique of 'contraction and release' revolutioni[sed] modern dancing and is still used today.

Martha Graham and her dance partner, Bertram Ross

The Martha Graham Dance Company performs.

Martha Graham revolutionised dance, lighting, stage designing, costuming, and music with her creative ideas. She gave her last performance at the age of 76 and choreographed 181 works over 60 years.

George Balanchine was born in Russia and choreographed his first dance whilst still a teenager. In 1924, he left Russia to move to the West to gain more creative freedom. He became a choreographer at the famous Ballet Russes dance company in Paris. In 1933, Balanchine moved to the USA and in 1948, his dance company officially became the New York City Ballet. He choreographed more than 400 dances and was the head of the company until his death in 1983.

a rare curtain call by George Balanchine

tribute to mark he Balanchine entennial (the 0th anniversary his birth)

Matthew Bourne

Matthew Bourne's male version of Swan Lake

ATTHEW BOURNE 1960–

atthew Bourne is a famous British ballet dancer and choreographer
orking today. He founded his own dance company in 1987 and created
ew version of the famous ballet, *Swan Lake*, in 1995. The traditionally
nale roles of the swans were all danced by men, which was controversial
d exciting. His *Swan Lake* featured in the closing scene of the 2000 film,
ly Elliott. He continues to create both adaptations and his own original
ce pieces, which his dance companies perform around the world.

WHO'S WHO IN A DANCE COMPANY

It takes more than a choreographer to create a dance performance. Here are some of the other people who might be involved.

Artistic director

This person is often also the choreographer. This person decides what shows to put on and casts the roles. The creative vision and direction of any company rests with its artistic director.

Artistic directors are responsible for the creative side of the business.

Dance teacher

The dance teacher runs daily classes and gives individual coaching to dancers. This person keeps everyone in shape and ready to go.

getting the moves right

Wardrobe supervisor

This job involves taking care of costumes, including any cleaning, repairing, and organising rental costumes.

Looking after all those clothes is a big job.

HOW MANY?

Dance companies vary widely in size. Small companies might have just an artistic director/choreographer, administrator and dancers. They then hire freelance staff when required or use the theatre staff where they're performing. At the other end of the scale, large companies could have all these staff, and many more!

Theatre & Dan

Technical director or stage manager

The technical director coordinates the dancers and stage crew at the performance venue. This person is responsible for making sure all technical equipment is clean and safe.

Stage crew

The crew look after the electrics, such as wiring and special effects. They also set up the scenery, lights, sound, props and rigging for a production.

WORKING BEHIND THE SCENES

It takes many people to stage a dance performance, most of whom you'll never see. Behind-the-scenes people might include:

- **lighting riggers and operators**
- electricians and carpenters
- **designers (costumes, set, sound etc.)**
- receptionists/administrators
- **physiotherapists.**

Dance shows can need a lot of equipment.

Marketing officer

A marketing officer orders posters and leaflets to advertise shows, and arranges media photo shoots, interviews etc. They also organise programs to sell at the performances.

There's always lots to do to promote dance shows.

General manager

This person arranges tour dates, everyone's salary, and handles all general business matters. They keep the company running from day to day.

Dancing professionally is tough on the body.

looking after the practical side of the business

19

the Creative Process

The initial idea for my choreography may come from anywhere – listening to music, watching people on the street, something I've read, or just my desire to express something particular.

I love to watch people going by.

Music can be inspiring.

I may work alone for a long time to build up the dance. Or I might get straight to work with my dancers, allowing them to help me develop my ideas.

I jot down ideas as they come to me.

There are many ways to choreograph.

Whilst I like to begin my creative process with improvising, there are many different ways to approach choreography. It can be a very structured process – with the steps carefully mapped out for the dancers to follow exactly, step-by-step. Or it might be a rough idea that the choreographer works on with the dancers to create the finished dance.

CAPOEIRA – DANCE FORM OR MARTIAL ART?

Capoeira is an African/Brazilian martial art that blends dance, music, singing and acrobatics. Modern capoeiristas jump, flip, turn and lunge to try to catch their partners off guard.

Capoeira in action.

I picture the dance floor as a clean slate and then make my mark on it.

I always tell my dancers to be open to different ways of working. Improvisation is a wonderful way to find fresh ideas. However, knowledge of dance techniques will help the creative process.

MODERN FEET

As opposed to ballet, which is about resisting gravity, modern dance uses the weight of the body in relation to the ground. Dancing in bare feet enables the dancer to connect directly with the floor. Over time, the soles of a dancer's feet adjust and toughen. Some modern dancers put tape on their toes and the balls of their feet to make it easier to turn and slide.

a modern dancer connecting to the floor

GET THE MESSAGE ACROSS

What is the dancer trying to say?

In order to choose an appropriate style for my choreography, I need to identify what I am trying to communicate to the audience.

DO I WANT TO TELL A STORY?

Literal (narrative) choreography

Dances that contain a message, or communicate a story to the audience, have literal choreography. In the early years of modern dance, it was traditional to design dances this way. Dancers used movements instead of words to tell stories. Many famous 19th century ballets, such as *The Nutcracker* or *Giselle*, tell clear stories.

Literal dances have a specific story to tell.

The Nutcracker ballet

DIDYOUKNOW?

TUMMY IMPROVISATION

Belly dancing is one of the most commonly improvised dances, since it is hard to follow structured choreography with the live music accompaniment. Professional belly dancers may dance six nights a week, up to three times a night, and simply do not have time to choreograph 15–60 minutes of dance for each night.

That's a lot of dancing!

There are about 200 dance companies in the UK and around 30,000 people are involved in dance related jobs from choreographers to teachers, from community development workers to therapists!

DO I WANT TO REPRESENT AN ESSENCE OR FEELING?

Choreography using abstraction or patterns

Whilst they don't tell a story, these dances still draw from life and contain the essence of real experience. For example, a dance containing an abstraction about the sea or seashore might contain dance movements that mimic movements of the sea. A dance that is an abstraction suggests the idea of something, not the thing directly. These dances may be used to express feelings, such as revenge, delight or freedom – or to create fantasy dances, as in the ballet *Concert*.

She's dancing about fire.

This dance is all about feelings.

Non-literal dances focus on movement.

DO I WANT TO EXPLORE MOVEMENT?

Non-literal choreography

These dances experiment with movement instead of telling a story. Whilst these are dances of mood, they are as structured and choreographed as any narrative dance. Examples include *Les Sylphides*, created by Mikhail Fokine in 1909, or *Jewels*, created by George Balanchine in 1967.

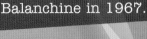

the famous non-literal ballet, *Les Sylphides*

Working the

As a choreographer, I must understand how dance movements work on stage. It's no good creating a beautiful dance in the studio that looks terrible when performed on a real stage. Here are some industry secrets to using a stage.

Centre stage is both the strongest and weakest part of the stage. For a climax it can be strong, but spend too much time there and the performance becomes dull and boring.

upstage right

Upstage corners are good for entrances.

upstage centre

centre stage

Coming forward in a straight line at the audience is confrontational. That's fine if the choreography intends that, but bad if it's accidental.

Corners have a sense of privacy – it's as if the audience is looking in on something.

downstage right

downstage centre

The very sides of the stage are very weak. Spending time there is not recommended.

upstage left

The middle of the side is the worst place to enter or exit – or to do anything at all, really.

downstage left

Downstage corners are good for exits.

STAGE TYPES

There are three main types of stage:

• proscenium stage – audience sits in rows in front of the stage, with the sides and back hidden from view

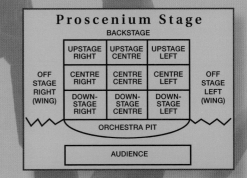

• thrust stage – audience sits in rows around three sides of the stage, with the backstage area still private

• arena stage/theatre-in-the-round – audience completely surrounds the stage and can see dancers coming on and off stage.

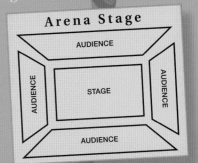

Shaping the dance

Choreographers use different musical structures to shape their dances.

AB

The AB form has two parts. First, part A presents a series of moves. Part B then presents a contrasting **theme**, e.g. the A form might be large movements and be performed high up, while the B form is slow and closer to the floor. The choreographer must create a smooth transition to move from one part to the other.

A B

Here's part A ...

... followed by part B.

ABA

The ABA is the same as AB, except after B, A is performed again but with a different twist. Again, skilful use of transition between the sections is needed.

A B A

SUITE

The typical suite has a moderate beginning, a slow second section and a fast, lively third section.

This time part A is a little different.

VARIATION TRICKS

A variation can be made by –

- changing the **tempo**, rhythm or direction of movements
- changing the structure, style or mood of the **theme**
- repeating or lengthening parts of the theme and leaving out other parts
- changing the number and placement of dancers.

This is an angry dance.

This would look very different with more dancers.

There might be solo dances too.

RONDO

In the Rondo, the A phrase is a repeated theme throughout the piece, with many different phrases in between, eg ABACADA, AEBACADA, ADADABAC, etc.

It takes great skill to plan a dance's themes and variations.

THEME AND VARIATIONS

A theme is presented, then repeated with changes, whilst still keeping the original theme recognisable. The theme is usually explored in several, different variations.

The theme can be a single phrase of movements or several movement phrases put together into a sequence.

The timing and movement of the original sequence must remain throughout the dance. Using themes and variations is both challenging and helpful to the choreographer, as it provides a framework within which to make movement choices.

New themes can be introduced for variety.

27

CHOREOGRAPHY SECRETS

Choreography theory can be studied at dance schools. I learnt my skills both by studying and by watching choreographers at work. I'm still learning now! There are some key ideas and tips that are valuable to know.

CAUTION! NON STOP MUSIC

Don't be a slave to the music – be guided by it, but feel free to use contrasting dance movements too.

Don't have your dancers turn their backs to an audience for too long. It's hard for the audience to stay connected to what's happening on stage if they are looking at people's backs.

Movements that feel fast and strong to a performer can appear slower and weaker to the audience watching. Check how the movements look, not just how they feel to you.

Circular movements are powerful on stage and should only be used when building up to the climax of a dance.

Always ask yourself, how will it look on stage?

Knowing when to stop is an important skill! It's easy to keep going when you're excited about the choreography. Beware of creating a dance that is too long – leave the audience wanting more!

It's time to wrap this up with a big finish.

The end of a dance carries a lot of its impact – it is a large part of what the audience remembers when they leave. Take time to create a good, strong ending.

And finally, remember to listen to good advice. If your dancers, or other choreographers, are telling you that something doesn't feel or look quite right, don't be too proud to take another look.

Be open to change.

DIDYOUKNOW?

INTERNATIONAL DANCE DAY

April 29, the birthday of famous French dancer and ballet master, Jean-Georges Noverre, is International Dance Day. Established in 1982, it seeks to raise awareness of the importance of dance and to encourage governments to include dance in their education systems.

Jean-Georges Noverre

Observing the dance

Choreographers must learn to look at the total picture they are attempting to create. It is our job to decide if a dance is working or not.

dance works!

- Are the moves dynamic, not static?

- Are dancers forming groups when they shouldn't be?

- Does each piece of the dance lead smoothly into the next?

That's definitely a dynamic move.

- Is there a sense of continuity?

- Is the dance interesting to watch?

These are just some of the many questions I must ask myself when watching a dance.

Recording the dance

There are several ways to record a dance, but I find filming it with a DVD camcorder is the simplest and easiest. I then sit and watch the dance over and over – this allows me to look at it with fresh eyes at different times.

Getting it down

Many choreographers use a combination of words, numbers, lines and stick figures to plan a dance or to remember what they have already worked out. Most big dance companies employ dance notators.

Excerpt from Giselle Act 1 Peasant pas de Deux Male Solo recorded in Benesh Movement Notation
Choreography after Coralli / Perrot / Petipa

This is what Benesh looks like.

There are two major dance notation systems – Labanotation and Benesh. Labanotation is used for all kinds of movement, while Benesh is mostly used for ballet. Both systems are logical, but complicated, and can be studied on dance courses at university. Since the 1920s, many famous dances have been written down, preserving them for future generations.

an excerpt of Labnotation

Title of dance: Sweet Low, Sweet Chariot from Negro Spirituals
Choreographer: Helen Tamiris
Notator: Lucy Venable
Courtesy of the Dance Notation Bureau

Computers and choreography

Some choreographers use computers to manipulate an image of a dancer on screen, or to record a phrase of movement and use the computer to build a dance around it. Computers can also store dances.

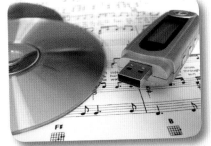

Modern technology is a huge help to choreographers.

Assessing the dance

When developing a dance, I like to assess it so I have a clear idea about what's working already and the areas that need more attention. I assess the dance with the following components, rating each with 10 as the highest score and 1 as the lowest.

Writing it down helps me focus.

Assessment sheet

1. Overall form of the dance – beginning, middle, end ☐

2. Unity, continuity, flow ☐

3. Variety, movement manipulation, sequence ☐

4. Repetition throughout overall dance ☐

5. Development of phrasing ☐

6. Relationship amongst dancers to express dance meaning ☐

7. Creative use of body shape ☐

That's a great body shape.

8. Use of stage: awareness of stage space, blocking, stage area, pathways ☐

9. Communication of purpose, feeling or solution of problem ☐

10. Performance, projection, aliveness of movement quality ☐

General Comments _____

Planning the performance

Planning a dance performance is a huge task. It helps to break it down into a series of smaller tasks, such as:

- auditions
- rehearsals
  - blocking rehearsals (working out the positions of dancers)
  - technical rehearsals (checking the props, lighting etc. work with the dance)
  - dress rehearsals (the final run-through in full costume)
- costume design
- stage and lighting design
- prop design
- design of promotion material
- promotion and marketing of the performance.

As a choreographer, it's vital for me to manage my time well so the dancers are ready on time. I must liaise with these other departments so they also have enough time to prepare the costumes, lights, programs etc. All these elements come together to make a performance out of a dance.

warming up for an audition

Working well with stage staff is important.

Rehearsals

Maybe that light's a bit bright?

Conditioning

Dancers and choreographers need to keep their bodies in peak (the best) condition, both to prevent injury and to dance their best. Dancers' bodies must be strong enough to cope with long hours of practice and performance.

Practice ...

... makes perfect.

If dancers don't warm up, they could hurt themselves.

Stretching and conditioning the body in training and rehearsals is often critical to the outcome and success of a performance.

24/7

Dancing is exhausting. Rehearsals require very long hours and usually take place daily, including weekends and holidays. If my company is on the road, we usually travel on weekends. Most performances are in the evenings, and we rehearse during the day. Dancers must also work late hours. It is important that choreographers understand and promote good body conditioning practices for their dancers.

Where are we performing tonight?

Dancers have to give 100 per cent for every performance.

Pilates

Pilates is a body conditioning method invented by Joseph Pilates in the 1920s. It emphasises flexibility and coordination and uses breathing techniques to help increase abdominal strength. Many well-known dancers include Pilates in their training as it encourages strength and control without adding bulk.

strength and control needed here

specialised Pilates equipment

ROYAL FOOTWORK

Queen Elizabeth I of England (1533–1603) reportedly danced the galliard for 20 minutes every morning to help keep her body in shape.

Elizabeth I

DIDYOUKNOW?

BEE WAGGLING

Waggle dance is a term used in beekeeping for a particular figure-of-eight dance of the honey bee. By performing this dance, bees share information with each other about the direction and distance to patches of flowers with nectar or pollen and to water sources.

Visualisation and imagery

One way choreographers can convey movement to dancers is through visualisation. Visualisation for a dancer is the ability to imagine an image in one's mind and then recreate that image in movement.

Today, I am beginning a series of visualisation and imagery exercises with my dancers. I ask them to imagine the early morning water lapping on the shore, turning into wild waves and then fun, playful surf. We begin to move around the studio as if we were the water, moving like the tides.

I then ask them to move across the studio sideways, with their knees bent like crabs, or to jump and dive like dolphins.

waking up at the beach

We imagine being squawking seagulls, sunbathers on the sand, and surfers on the waves – all the while being aware of the rhythm and beats of the music in the background. It helps get us all in the right frame of mind to communicate the life of a beach through the dances I've created.

fun at the beach

Can you move like a seagull?

It's quiet again.

36

USING THE SPACE

Movement may be directed:
- **forwards, backwards, sideways**
- **diagonally, circularly**
- **up, down.**

forwards

down

diagonally

Combining directions results in patterns like:
- **zigzag lines**
- **right angles**
- **squares**
- **arcs.**

The dancers could move at right angles to each other.

How about a square pattern?

Movement may be presented on different levels:
- **on the floor – sitting, kneeling, standing, jumping**
- **on different planes – horizontal, vertical.**

vertical dancing

horizontal dancing

Rehearsals

There are practical factors which affect the quality of any performance. Getting enough rehearsal time is fundamental. If the dancers are not ready, the performance will suffer. The dancers must also have the appropriate technical skills to fulfil the demands of the choreography.

With that in mind, I have worked out a rehearsal plan which I believe will get us ready for the big day without wearing everyone out beforehand. I've carefully considered how to use each dancer's skills in the best way.

For a dancer, practice never ends.

I pin up a schedule for the next six weeks on the studio noticeboard for everyone to see. We will have four rehearsal days per week leading up to the performance. On the weekend and day before the show, there will be full dress rehearsals on the venue stage.

Each of the three dances will have its own group. Two of my most skilled dancers will perform in both the first and the last dance.

After the first two rehearsals, I finalise the positioning of all the dancers.

Countdown to the show

Apart from the rehearsals, there are lots of other jobs to be done. Costumes have to be ordered, and each dancer has two costume fittings. I meet with the lighting designer to discuss the lighting colours and sequences we will use to create mood and atmosphere on the stage.

The lights set the mood.

A photographer and journalist come to the studio to promote the studio and our work. Without an audience, there is no performance! I provide feedback on the artwork for the posters and flyers announcing the event. The good news comes in a few weeks later that tickets are selling fast.

the beginning of a costume

In the afternoon I meet with the stage manager to go through the programme and double-check the stage space for our performance. I give make-up instructions to the dancers as they will be responsible for their own make-up. Both the dancers and everyone else involved need to have energy and focus to make the performance shine. It's up to me to keep everyone motivated and on track.

The photographer gets his shots.

ShoWtime!

1 HOUR BEFORE CURTAIN UP
The dancers arrive, change into their costumes in the dressing rooms and do warm-up exercises.

35 MINS TO GO
The dancers touch up their make-up.

15 MINS TO GO
The stage manager gives the dancers their 15 minute warning.

10 MINS BEFORE
Individual dance groups assemble at the back of the stage.

5 MINS BEFORE
The stage manager calls, "Group one, this is your call!" The first group takes its place in the wings of the stage.

1 MIN BEFORE
The stage manager **cues** the lighting operator and the lights dim.

15 SECONDS BEFORE
The lights fade to black ...

Here we are!

Kate gets ready.

It's a full house, wow!

Matt brings the lights down.

It's nerve-racking waiting in the wings.

ZERO!
Curtain up!

The music begins as the stage gently lights up in a soft, orange morning glow and the first group takes to the stage.

Backstage, the atmosphere is electric. We watch breathlessly as the performers begin to dance. It's unfolding just as I had planned. But I've still got my heart in my mouth as each dance leads effortlessly into the next, showing a day in the life of a beach.

We start with dawn … the slow awakening of the beach, the tide coming in, and the creatures stirring.

And finally, sunset … the water cools and quietens, the crowds go home and the beach's wildlife wind down for the night.

As the lights fade to depict the setting sun, the audience begins to clap. The dancers receive a standing ovation!

The performance is a huge success. All the hard work has been worth it. I am over the moon and so proud of my dancers! Choreographing a successful show is a wonderful, creative high — I'd recommend it to anyone!

The day ends.

The sky is grey as everything wakes up.

Take a bow.

Moving onto midday … it's all dazzling sunshine, fun and liveliness.

The seagulls soar in the sky.

The birds look for food.

The crabs scurry across the sand.

41

FOLLOW THESE STEPS TO BECOME A CHOREOGRAPHER

1. You will need a high level of dance training and experience, so dance as much as you can!

2. Most dancers begin formal training very young – between 5 and 15 years old – and often take graded examinations before going on to vocational training or higher education.

3. If there is a dance school in your local area, join and experience as many forms of dance as you can.

4. Join a dance group, or form your own, to provide you with the freedom and flexibility to create and perform your own work.

5. Keep creating! There are many different arenas for a choreographer to work in away from the stage, including film, music videos, fashion shows, sport or corporate events, or as a movement coach for actors and singers.

REMEMBER: Almost all choreographers begin their careers as dancers and usually start choreographing while still performing, especially in smaller companies.

dance teacher

DIDYOUKNOW?

There are around 22 dance colleges offering professional dance training courses accredited by the Council for Dance Education and Training and over 292 university courses with dance as a subject area.

Get your dancing shoes on!

Start young
if you can ...
boys too!

Making up routines
with your friends is
great practice . . .
and fun!

6. Choreographers need knowledge in many areas of the arts, so it is important to also have an interest in music, art and design.

7. There are a wide range of dance qualifications available including GCSE, A levels / H grades, GNVQ Advanced or BTEC National Certificates and Diplomas in Performing Arts or Dance.

8. At 18 you could train as a dancer at a vocational dance school, by taking a three-year degree/diploma in professional dance or musical theatre.

9. Several universities also offer degrees in dance, and some courses specialise in choreography.

Ask your Connexions PA, Careers Adviser or teacher for more details.

DIDYOUKNOW?

BRITAIN'S GOT TALENT!

In 2009, Diversity, a street dance group, won the third series of *Britain's Got Talent*. The troupe, from London and Essex, are three sets of brothers and four of their friends aged 12 to 26. Some are still at school or university but the older members include an IT systems engineer, a bathroom installer, and a telecoms engineer. The group's leader and choreographer is Ashley Banjo.

43

Opportunities for choreographers and other related areas

In many dance companies, dancers can contribute their own choreographic ideas. There are also a variety of other jobs that involve choreography in some way.

- ✓ Community dance worker – working with communities to facilitate the expression of that group's ideas in dance.

- ✓ Dance teacher – teaching at dance studios, or owning and running a dancing school (dancers with appropriate qualifications can teach in secondary schools or tertiary institutions).

- ✓ Dance therapist – using dance as part of a therapy programme for a wide range of people, including the elderly, or children and adults with special needs or specific movement disabilities.

You are most likely to work freelance on fixed-term contracts, although there are some full-time permanent opportunities. You would mainly work in dance studios and rehearsal rooms, but also in theatres, film and TV studios, nightclubs, halls and holiday centres.

Many dance jobs are based in London, but you could also work for regional dance organisations, touring productions, or abroad.

What will I earn?

Starting salaries for dancers moving into choreography are around £20,000 a year. Once established, earnings can reach £40,000 or more.

Useful contacts

Dance UK www.danceuk.org
Dance UK offers information and advice through the National Choreographers' Forum.
The Urdang, The Old Finsbury Town Hall, Rosebery Avenue, London EC1R 4QT
Tel: 020 7713 0730

Council for Dance Education and Training (CDET) www.cdet.org.uk
Lists dance colleges across the UK.
Old Brewer's Yard, 17-19 Neal Street, Covent Garden, London WC2H 9UY
Tel: 020 7240 5703

The All England Dance Association www.all-england-dance.co.uk
The All England Dance Association hold a Young Dancer of the Year and Young Tap Dancer of the Year competition. For further details go to their website or write to: PO Box 518, Torquay TQ1 9EN   Tel: 01803 607414

For further information about dance festivals across the UK and internationally go to: www.danceeurope.net

Dancers Pro www.uk.dancerspro.com
Useful industry guides and tips on training and building your career.

Creative Choices www.creative-choices.co.uk
Information about becoming a choreographer and gives real life examples in performing arts.

Skillset Careers www.skillset.org/careers
Information and advice on choreography and dance careers.
Tel: 08080 300 900 (England and Northern Ireland)
0808 100 8094 (Scotland) 0800 0121 815 (Wales)

The Stage www.thestage.co.uk
The entertainment trade weekly newspaper, including recruitment advertisements, useful links, and 'how to guides'.

Contacts www.spotlight.com
Published annually by The Spotlight, this book provides details of all aspects of the entertainment industry.

Glossary

adaptations – things that have been changed or adjusted from their original versions

artefacts – useful objects made by humans

choreograph – design dance steps

classical – traditional

commissioned – asked someone else to undertake a task

contemporary – modern; existing now

controversial – something that causes a lot of discussion or argument

cues – signals for a performer, telling them when to begin

curtain call – when a performer take another bow on stage in response to audience applause

dynamic – full of energy and new ideas

essence – most important part of something; the nature of something

flamenco – type of lively, Spanish dance and music

freelance – someone who does not work for a company on a regular basis, but is paid for each individual job they complete

galliard – lively dance for two dancers, popular in the 16th and 17th centuries

indigenous – native to a particular country

kinaesthetic – awareness of movement and position of the body

literal – most basic meaning; true to fact

manipulate – to influence or change something

percussive – featuring or sounding like percussion instruments, such as a drum or a cymbal

pioneer – someone who first explores an area or idea, opening the way for others

pointe – very tip of the toe

spatial – relating to space

tempo – speed and rhythm

theme – main idea or subject

Index

other titles in the series

 **PILOT**

 **FORENSIC SCIENTIST**

 **TV PRODUCER**

 **MAGAZINE EDITOR**

 **GAME DEVELOPER**

 **MOTOR MECHANIC**

 **ANIMATOR**

 **BUILDER**

 **CHEF**

 **SPORTS TRAINER**

 **FASHION DESIGNER**

 **FIRE FIGHTER**

 **ZOO KEEPER**

 **MARINE BIOLOGIST**

 **LAWYER**